Borders, Citizenship and Immigration Act 2009

CHAPTER 11

Explanatory Notes are available separately

GRAN*GIS* UK Publishing

Adapted and published by GRANGIS (Grand Register Library).
Online: www.grangis.com
E-mail: contact@grangis.com

In this version:
ISBN: 979-8-88559-058-7

Note: This is the original version (as it was originally enacted). Title, sub-title and the generated date is as marked on the pages.

Borders, Citizenship and Immigration Act 2009

CHAPTER 11

BORDERS, CITIZENSHIP AND IMMIGRATION ACT 2009

PART 1

BORDER FUNCTIONS

General customs functions of the Secretary of State

General customs officials

The Director of Border Revenue

Customs revenue officials

Use and disclosure of information

Investigations and detention

Transfer of property etc.

Inspection and oversight

Other provisions

Supplementary

PART 2

CITIZENSHIP

Acquisition of British citizenship by naturalisation

Acquisition of British citizenship by birth

Borders, Citizenship and Immigration Act 2009

2009 CHAPTER 11

An Act to provide for customs functions to be exercisable by the Secretary of State, the Director of Border Revenue and officials designated by them; to make provision about the use and disclosure of customs information; to make provision for and in connection with the exercise of customs functions and functions relating to immigration, asylum or nationality; to make provision about citizenship and other nationality matters; to make further provision about immigration and asylum; and for connected purposes. [21st July 2009]

BE IT ENACTED by the Queen's most Excellent Majesty, by and with the advice and consent of the Lords Spiritual and Temporal, and Commons, in this present Parliament assembled, and by the authority of the same, as follows:—

PART 1

BORDER FUNCTIONS

General customs functions of the Secretary of State

1 General customs functions of the Secretary of State

(1) The functions of the Commissioners for Her Majesty's Revenue and Customs that are exercisable in relation to general customs matters are exercisable by the Secretary of State concurrently with the Commissioners.

(2) For the purposes of this Part, a "general customs matter" is a matter in relation to which the Commissioners, or officers of Revenue and Customs, have functions, other than—

(a) a matter listed in Schedule 1 to the Commissioners for Revenue and Customs Act 2005 (c. 11),

(b) any tax, duty or levy not mentioned in that Schedule,

(c) a matter in respect of which functions were transferred to the Commissioners from the Paymaster General under the Transfer of Functions (Office of Her Majesty's Paymaster General) Order 2006 (S.I. 2006/607),

(d) the subject matter of Directive 2005/60/EC on the prevention of the use of the financial system for the purpose of money laundering and terrorist financing (as amended from time to time), and

(e) the subject matter of Regulation (EC) No 1781/2006 on information on the payer accompanying transfers of funds (as amended from time to time).

(3) If a function is exercisable by the Commissioners—

(a) in relation to a general customs matter, and

(b) in relation to any other matter,

the function is exercisable by the Secretary of State in relation to the general customs matter only.

(4) So far as is appropriate for the purposes of or in connection with this section, references to the Commissioners for Her Majesty's Revenue and Customs, or to Her Majesty's Revenue and Customs, in an enactment, instrument or document to which this section applies are to be construed as including a reference to the Secretary of State.

(5) References in this section (other than in subsection (8))—

(a) to functions of the Commissioners are to functions conferred by an enactment to which this section applies;

(b) to functions of officers of Revenue and Customs are to functions conferred by an enactment to which section 3 (designation of general customs officials) applies.

(6) This section applies to—

(a) an enactment passed or made before the end of the session in which this Act is passed, and

(b) an instrument or document issued before the passing of this Act.

(7) This includes—

(a) section 5(2)(b) of the Commissioners for Revenue and Customs Act 2005 (c. 11) (Commissioners' initial functions),

(b) section 9 of that Act (ancillary powers),

(c) section 25A(2) of that Act (certificates of debt),

(d) section 31 of that Act (obstruction), and

(e) section 33 of that Act (power of arrest) other than in its application to an offence under section 30 of that Act (impersonation),

but does not include any other enactment contained in that Act.

(8) In this Part "general customs function" means—

(a) a function that is exercisable—

(i) by the Secretary of State by virtue of this section, or

(ii) by general customs officials by virtue of section 3,

(b) a function that is conferred on general customs officials or the Secretary of State by or by virtue of any of sections 22 to 24 (investigations and detention), or

(c) a function under Community law that is exercisable by the Secretary of State or general customs officials in relation to a matter—
 (i) in relation to which functions under Community law are exercisable by the Commissioners or officers of Revenue and Customs, and
 (ii) that is not listed in paragraphs (a) to (e) of subsection (2).

2 Power of Secretary of State to modify functions

(1) The Secretary of State may by order—
 (a) amend section 1(2) (matters that are general customs matters) so as to add, modify or remove a matter;
 (b) amend that section so as to exclude its application in relation to a function of the Commissioners for Her Majesty's Revenue and Customs or to modify or remove a reference to a function previously so excluded;
 (c) make provision for that section to apply in relation to a function conferred on the Commissioners by an enactment passed or made after the end of the session in which this Act is passed;
 (d) modify any enactment (including an enactment passed or made after the passing of this Act) in consequence of provision made under any of paragraphs (a) to (c);
 (e) make provision for a function of the Secretary of State or general customs officials to be treated, or not to be treated, as a general customs function.

(2) The power under subsection (1)(a) may not be exercised to add any of the following to section 1(2)—
 (a) a matter listed in Schedule 1 to the Commissioners for Revenue and Customs Act 2005 (c. 11),
 (b) value added tax,
 (c) a customs revenue matter (as to which, see section 7), or
 (d) a matter listed at section 7(2)(e).

(3) The Secretary of State must consult the Treasury before exercising the power under this section.

General customs officials

3 Designation of general customs officials

(1) The Secretary of State by whom general customs functions are exercisable may designate—
 (a) an immigration officer, or
 (b) any other official in that Secretary of State's department,
 as a general customs official.

(2) A general customs official—
 (a) has, in relation to a general customs matter, the same functions as an officer of Revenue and Customs would have, and
 (b) may exercise the functions conferred on the Secretary of State by section 1 (general customs functions of the Secretary of State).

(3) This does not prevent the exercise of the Secretary of State's functions by any other official of the Secretary of State.

(4) If a function within subsection (2) is exercisable—

(a) in relation to a general customs matter, and

(b) in relation to any other matter,

the function is exercisable by a general customs official in relation to the general customs matter only.

(5) So far as is appropriate for the purposes of or in connection with this section, references to an officer of Revenue and Customs, or to Her Majesty's Revenue and Customs, in an enactment, instrument or document to which this section applies are to be construed as including a reference to a general customs official.

(6) References in this section to functions of an officer of Revenue and Customs are to functions conferred by an enactment to which this section applies.

(7) This section applies to—

(a) an enactment passed or made, or an instrument or document issued, before this Act is passed, and

(b) subject to express provision to the contrary, an enactment passed or made, or an instrument or document issued, after this Act is passed.

(8) This includes—

(a) section 2(4) of the Commissioners for Revenue and Customs Act 2005 (c. 11) (continuation of anything begun by one officer by another),

(b) section 6 of that Act (officers' initial functions),

(c) section 25(1) and (5) of that Act (conduct of civil proceedings in a magistrates' court or in the sheriff court),

(d) section 25A(1) of that Act (certificates of debt),

(e) section 31 of that Act (obstruction),

(f) section 32 of that Act (assault), and

(g) section 33 of that Act (power of arrest) other than in its application to an offence under section 30 of that Act (impersonation),

but does not otherwise include any enactment contained in that Act.

(9) This section has effect subject to—

(a) any limitation specified in the official's designation under section 4 (supplementary provisions about designation), and

(b) any designation of the official under section 11 (designation of customs revenue officials).

4 Designation: supplementary

(1) A designation under section 3 is subject to such limitations as may be specified in the designation.

(2) A limitation specified under subsection (1) may, in particular, relate to—

(a) the functions that are exercisable by virtue of the designation, or

(b) the purposes for which those functions are exercisable.

(3) A designation under section 3—

(a) may be permanent or for a specified period,
(b) may (in either case) be withdrawn, and
(c) may be varied.

(4) The power to designate, or to withdraw or vary a designation, is exercised by the Secretary of State giving notice to the official in question.

(5) The Secretary of State may designate an official under section 3 only if the Secretary of State is satisfied that the official—
(a) is capable of effectively carrying out the functions that are exercisable by virtue of the designation,
(b) has received adequate training in respect of the exercise of those functions, and
(c) is otherwise a suitable person to exercise those functions.

5 Directions by the Secretary of State

A general customs official must comply with the directions of the Secretary of State in the exercise of general customs functions.

The Director of Border Revenue

6 The Director of Border Revenue

(1) The Secretary of State must designate an official in the department of the Secretary of State by whom general customs functions are exercisable as the Director of Border Revenue.

(2) Before making a designation under this section, the Secretary of State must obtain the consent of the Treasury to the designation.

7 Customs revenue functions of the Director

(1) The functions of the Commissioners for Her Majesty's Revenue and Customs that are exercisable in relation to customs revenue matters are exercisable by the Director of Border Revenue concurrently with the Commissioners.

(2) For the purposes of this Part, each of the following is a "customs revenue matter"—
(a) agricultural levies (within the meaning given by section 6(8) of the European Communities Act 1972 (c. 68));
(b) anti-dumping duty (within the meaning of Council Regulation (EC) No. 384/96, as amended from time to time);
(c) countervailing duty (within the meaning of Council Regulation (EC) No. 2026/97, as amended from time to time);
(d) customs duties;
(e) duties of excise other than—
(i) amusement machine licence duty,
(ii) bingo duty,
(iii) gaming duty,
(iv) general betting duty,

Status: This is the original version (as it was originally enacted).

(v) lottery duty,

(vi) pool betting duty, and

(vii) remote gaming duty;

(f) value added tax so far as relating to the export of goods from, or the import of goods into, the United Kingdom.

(3) Subsection (1) does not apply to—

(a) any function of making, by statutory instrument, any regulations, rules or an order;

(b) any function of issuing notices, directions or conditions that relate to value added tax and that apply generally to any person falling within their terms.

(4) If a function is exercisable by the Commissioners—

(a) in relation to a customs revenue matter, and

(b) in relation to any other matter,

the function is exercisable by the Director in relation to the customs revenue matter only.

(5) So far as is appropriate for the purposes of or in connection with this section, references to the Commissioners for Her Majesty's Revenue and Customs, or to Her Majesty's Revenue and Customs, in an enactment, instrument or document to which this section applies are to be construed as including a reference to the Director.

(6) References in this section to functions of the Commissioners are to functions conferred by an enactment to which this section applies.

(7) This section applies to—

(a) an enactment passed or made before the end of the session in which this Act is passed, and

(b) an instrument or document issued before the passing of this Act.

(8) This includes—

(a) section 5(1)(b) and (2)(b) of the Commissioners for Revenue and Customs Act 2005 (c. 11) (Commissioners' initial functions),

(b) section 9 of that Act (ancillary powers),

(c) section 24(1), (2), (3)(e) and (4) to (7) of that Act (evidence),

(d) section 25(1), (1A), (5) and (6) of that Act (conduct of civil proceedings),

(e) section 25A(2) of that Act (certificates of debt),

(f) section 26 of that Act (rewards),

(g) section 31 of that Act (obstruction), and

(h) section 33 of that Act (power of arrest) other than in its application to an offence under section 30 of that Act (impersonation),

but does not include any other enactment contained in that Act.

(9) In this Part "customs revenue function" means—

(a) a function that is exercisable—

(i) by the Director by virtue of this section, or

(ii) by customs revenue officials by virtue of section 11,

(b) a function that is conferred on customs revenue officials or the Director by or by virtue of any of sections 22 to 24 (investigations and detention), or

(c) a function under Community law that is exercisable by the Director or customs revenue officials in relation to a customs revenue matter.

8 Power of Treasury to modify Director's functions

The Treasury may by order—

(a) amend section 7(2) (matters that are customs revenue matters) so as to add, modify or remove a matter;

(b) amend section 7(3) (functions to which that section does not apply) so as to add, modify or remove a function;

(c) make provision for that section to apply in relation to a function conferred on the Commissioners for Her Majesty's Revenue and Customs by an enactment passed or made after the end of the session in which this Act is passed;

(d) modify any enactment (including an enactment passed or made after the passing of this Act) in consequence of provision made under any of paragraphs (a) to (c).

9 Delegation of Director's functions

(1) The Director of Border Revenue may make arrangements to delegate a function of the Director.

(2) The delegation of a function under this section—

(a) does not prevent the exercise of the function by the Director, and

(b) does not prevent the exercise of the function by a customs revenue official (see section 11).

(3) Where the Director delegates a function under this section—

(a) the Director must monitor the exercise of the function by the person to whom it is delegated, and

(b) the person must comply with the directions of the Director in exercising that function.

10 Compliance with directions etc.

(1) This section applies to—

(a) the Director of Border Revenue in the exercise of the Director's customs revenue functions, and

(b) a person to whom such functions are delegated under section 9.

(2) A person to whom this section applies must comply with any directions of a general nature given by the Treasury.

(3) A person to whom this section applies must apply—

(a) any concession published by the Commissioners for Her Majesty's Revenue and Customs and available generally to any person falling within its terms, and

(b) any interpretation of the law issued by the Commissioners (whether or not published).

(4) A person to whom this section applies must also—

(a) comply with any other guidance issued by the Commissioners (whether or not published), and

(b) take account of any other material published by the Commissioners.

Customs revenue officials

11 Designation of customs revenue officials

(1) The Director of Border Revenue may designate—

(a) an immigration officer, or

(b) any other official in the department of the Secretary of State by whom general customs functions are exercisable,

as a customs revenue official.

(2) A customs revenue official—

(a) has, in relation to a customs revenue matter, the same functions as an officer of Revenue and Customs would have, and

(b) may exercise the functions conferred on the Director by section 7 (customs revenue functions).

(3) If a function within subsection (2) is exercisable—

(a) in relation to a customs revenue matter, and

(b) in relation to any other matter,

the function is exercisable by a customs revenue official in relation to the customs revenue matter only.

(4) So far as is appropriate for the purposes of or in connection with this section, references to an officer of Revenue and Customs, or to Her Majesty's Revenue and Customs, in an enactment, instrument or document to which this section applies are to be construed as including a reference to a customs revenue official.

(5) References in this section to functions of an officer of Revenue and Customs are to functions conferred by an enactment to which this section applies.

(6) This section applies to—

(a) an enactment passed or made, or an instrument or document issued, before this Act is passed, and

(b) subject to express provision to the contrary, an enactment passed or made, or an instrument or document issued, after this Act is passed.

(7) This includes—

(a) section 2(4) of the Commissioners for Revenue and Customs Act 2005 (c. 11) (continuation of anything begun by one officer by another),

(b) section 6 of that Act (officers' initial functions),

(c) section 25(1), (1A) and (5) of that Act (conduct of civil proceedings),

(d) section 25A(1) of that Act (certificates of debt),

(e) section 26 of that Act (rewards),

(f) section 31 of that Act (obstruction),

(g) section 32 of that Act (assault), and

(h) section 33 of that Act (power of arrest) other than in its application to an offence under section 30 of that Act (impersonation),

but does not otherwise include any enactment contained in that Act.

(8) This section has effect subject to—
(a) any limitation specified in the official's designation under section 12 (supplementary provisions about designation), and
(b) any designation of the official under section 3 (designation of general customs officials).

12 Designation: supplementary

(1) A designation under section 11 is subject to such limitations as may be specified in the designation.

(2) A limitation specified under subsection (1) may, in particular, relate to—
(a) the functions that are exercisable by virtue of the designation, or
(b) the purposes for which those functions are exercisable.

(3) A designation under section 11—
(a) may be permanent or for a specified period,
(b) may (in either case) be withdrawn, and
(c) may be varied.

(4) The power to designate, or to withdraw or vary a designation, is exercised by the Director of Border Revenue giving notice to the official in question.

(5) The Director may designate an official under section 11 only if the Director is satisfied that the official—
(a) is capable of effectively carrying out the functions that are exercisable by virtue of the designation,
(b) has received adequate training in respect of the exercise of those functions, and
(c) is otherwise a suitable person to exercise those functions.

13 Directions by the Director

A customs revenue official must comply with the directions of the Director of Border Revenue in the exercise of customs revenue functions.

Use and disclosure of information

14 Use and disclosure of customs information

(1) A person to whom this section applies may—
(a) use customs information acquired by that person in connection with a function exercisable by that person for the purpose of any other function exercisable by that person, and
(b) disclose customs information to any other person to whom this section applies for the purpose of a function exercisable by that person.

(2) The persons to whom this section applies are—
(a) a designated customs official,
(b) an immigration officer,

(c) the Secretary of State by whom general customs functions are exercisable,
(d) any other Minister of the Crown in the department of that Secretary of State,
(e) the Director of Border Revenue, and
(f) a person acting on behalf of a person mentioned in paragraphs (a) to (e).

(3) This section is subject to any provision that restricts or prohibits the use or disclosure of information and that is contained in—
(a) this Part,
(b) any other enactment, or
(c) an international or other agreement to which the United Kingdom or Her Majesty's Government is party.

(4) In subsection (3) the reference to an enactment does not include an enactment contained in, or in an instrument made under—
(a) an Act of the Scottish Parliament,
(b) a Measure or Act of the National Assembly for Wales, or
(c) Northern Ireland legislation.

(5) This section is without prejudice to—
(a) the use by a person to whom it applies of information other than customs information;
(b) the disclosure by or to a person to whom it applies of information other than customs information.

(6) In this Part—

"customs function" means a general customs function or a customs revenue function;

"customs information" means information acquired or capable of being acquired as a result of the exercise of a customs function;

"customs revenue information" means information acquired or capable of being acquired as a result of the exercise of a customs revenue function;

"designated customs official" means a general customs official or a customs revenue official.

(7) It is immaterial for the purposes of subsection (6)—
(a) whether the information was acquired or is capable of being acquired by the person by whom it is held or another person;
(b) whether the information was also acquired or is also capable of being acquired in the exercise of any other function.

15 Prohibition on disclosure of personal customs information

(1) A person who is or was a relevant official, the Secretary of State by whom general customs functions are exercisable or another Minister of the Crown in that Secretary of State's department may not disclose personal customs information to a person who is not—
(a) a relevant official, or
(b) a Minister of the Crown in that department.

(2) A person who is or was a relevant official may not disclose personal customs revenue information to a Minister of the Crown.

(3) In this Part "relevant official" means—

(a) a designated customs official,

(b) an immigration officer,

(c) the Director of Border Revenue, or

(d) a person acting on behalf of—

(i) the Secretary of State by whom general customs functions are exercisable, or

(ii) a person mentioned in paragraphs (a) to (c).

(4) In this Part—

"personal customs information" means customs information relating to a person that—

(a) identifies that person, or

(b) enables that person to be identified (either by itself or in combination with other information);

"personal customs revenue information" means customs revenue information relating to a person that—

(a) identifies that person, or

(b) enables that person to be identified (either by itself or in combination with other information).

(5) A person—

(a) does not breach subsection (1) by disclosing information the person knows was acquired otherwise than as the result of the exercise of a customs function;

(b) does not breach subsection (2) by disclosing information the person knows was acquired otherwise than as the result of the exercise of a customs revenue function.

(6) Subsections (1) and (2) are also subject to—

(a) section 16 (exceptions to the prohibition in this section), and

(b) any enactment (other than an enactment contained in this Part) permitting disclosure, where the disclosure in question does not contravene any restriction imposed by the Commissioners for Her Majesty's Revenue and Customs on the disclosure of customs revenue information.

(7) This section does not apply to information supplied by or on behalf of Her Majesty's Revenue and Customs or the Revenue and Customs Prosecutions Office.

This is without prejudice to any other restriction on the disclosure of such information.

(8) In subsection (6) the reference to an enactment does not include an enactment contained in, or in an instrument made under—

(a) an Act of the Scottish Parliament,

(b) a Measure or Act of the National Assembly for Wales, or

(c) Northern Ireland legislation.

16 Exceptions to section 15 prohibition

(1) A person does not breach section 15(1) or (2) by making a disclosure—

(a) to which any of subsections (3) to (8) applies, and

(b) which, in the case of a disclosure of customs revenue information, does not contravene any restriction imposed by the Commissioners for Her Majesty's Revenue and Customs.

(2) Subsection (1)(b) does not apply if the person making the disclosure knows that the information was acquired otherwise than as the result of the exercise of a customs revenue function.

(3) This subsection applies to a disclosure which is made for the purposes of—

(a) a customs function,

(b) a function relating to immigration, asylum or nationality,

(c) a function relating to national security, or

(d) a function relating to the prevention or detection of crime.

(4) This subsection applies to a disclosure which is made to a person exercising public functions (whether or not within the United Kingdom) for the purposes of any of those functions.

(5) This subsection applies to a disclosure which—

(a) is made for the purposes of civil proceedings (whether or not within the United Kingdom) relating to a function within subsection (3),

(b) is made for the purposes of a criminal investigation or criminal proceedings (whether or not within the United Kingdom), or

(c) is made in pursuance of an order of a court.

(6) This subsection applies to a disclosure which is made with the consent of each person to whom the information relates.

(7) This subsection applies to a disclosure which is made in order to comply with an obligation of the United Kingdom, or Her Majesty's Government, under an international or other agreement.

(8) This subsection applies to a disclosure—

(a) to a person specified in regulations made jointly by the Treasury and the Secretary of State, or

(b) of a kind specified in such regulations.

17 Prohibition on further disclosure

(1) A person to whom information is disclosed in reliance on section 16 or this section may not disclose that information without the consent of a relevant official (which may be general or specific).

(2) A person does not breach subsection (1) by making a disclosure—

(a) to which any of subsections (3) to (8) of section 16 applies, and

(b) which, in the case of a disclosure of customs revenue information, does not contravene any restriction imposed by the Commissioners for Her Majesty's Revenue and Customs.

(3) Subsection (2)(b) does not apply if the person making the disclosure knows that the information was acquired otherwise than as the result of the exercise of a customs revenue function.

(4) This section is also subject to any other enactment permitting disclosure.

(5) In subsection (4) the reference to an enactment does not include an enactment contained in, or in an instrument made under—

(a) an Act of the Scottish Parliament,

(b) a Measure or Act of the National Assembly for Wales, or

(c) Northern Ireland legislation.

18 Offence of wrongful disclosure

(1) A person commits an offence if the person breaches section 15(1) or (2) or 17(1).

(2) It is a defence for a person charged with an offence under this section to prove that the person reasonably believed—

(a) that the disclosure was lawful, or

(b) that the information had already and lawfully been made available to the public.

(3) A prosecution for an offence under this section—

(a) may be brought in England and Wales only with the consent of the Director of Public Prosecutions or the Director of Revenue and Customs Prosecutions;

(b) may be brought in Northern Ireland only with the consent of the Director of Public Prosecutions for Northern Ireland.

(4) This section is without prejudice to the pursuit of any remedy or the taking of any action in relation to a breach of section 15(1) or (2) or 17(1) (whether or not this section applies to the breach).

(5) A person guilty of an offence under this section is liable—

(a) on conviction on indictment to imprisonment for a term not exceeding 2 years, or to a fine, or to both;

(b) on summary conviction—

(i) in England and Wales, to imprisonment for a term not exceeding 12 months, or to a fine not exceeding the statutory maximum, or to both;

(ii) in Scotland, to imprisonment for a term not exceeding 12 months, or to a fine not exceeding the statutory maximum, or to both;

(iii) in Northern Ireland, to imprisonment for a term not exceeding 6 months, or to a fine not exceeding the statutory maximum, or to both.

(6) In relation to an offence under this section committed before the commencement of section 282 of the Criminal Justice Act 2003 (c. 44) (increase in maximum sentence on summary conviction of offence triable either way), the reference in subsection (5)(b)(i) to 12 months has effect as if it were a reference to 6 months.

19 Application of statutory provisions

(1) Nothing in sections 14 to 17 authorises the making of a disclosure which—

(a) contravenes the Data Protection Act 1998 (c. 29), or

(b) is prohibited by Part 1 of the Regulation of Investigatory Powers Act 2000 (c. 23).

(2) Information whose disclosure is prohibited by section 15(1) or (2) or 17(1) is exempt information by virtue of section 44(1)(a) of the Freedom of Information Act 2000 (c. 36).

(3) Sections 15(6), 16 and 17(2) and (4) are to be disregarded in determining for the purposes of subsection (2) whether the disclosure of personal customs information is prohibited by section 15(1) or (2) or 17(1).

(4) In section 23 of the Commissioners for Revenue and Customs Act 2005 (c. 11) (freedom of information), after subsection (1) insert—

"(1A) Subsections (2) and (3) of section 18 are to be disregarded in determining for the purposes of subsection (1) of this section whether the disclosure of revenue and customs information relating to a person is prohibited by subsection (1) of that section."

20 Supply of Revenue and Customs information

(1) After section 41 of the UK Borders Act 2007 (c. 30) insert—

"41A Supply of information to UK Border Agency

(1) HMRC and the RCPO may each supply a person to whom this section applies with information for use for the purpose of the customs functions exercisable by that person.

(2) This section applies to—

(a) a designated customs official,

(b) the Secretary of State by whom general customs functions are exercisable,

(c) the Director of Border Revenue, and

(d) a person acting on behalf of a person mentioned in paragraphs (a) to (c).

(3) This section applies to a document or article which comes into the possession of, or is discovered by, HMRC or the RCPO, or a person acting on behalf of HMRC or the RCPO, as it applies to information.

(4) A person to whom this section applies—

(a) may retain for a purpose within subsection (1) a document or article supplied by virtue of subsection (3);

(b) may dispose of a document or article supplied by virtue of subsection (3).

(5) A power conferred by this section on HMRC or the RCPO may be exercised on behalf of HMRC or the RCPO by a person who is authorised (generally or specifically) for the purpose.

(6) In this section and section 41B "customs function" and "general customs function" have the meanings given by Part 1 of the Borders, Citizenship and Immigration Act 2009.

41B UK Border Agency: onward disclosure

(1) A person to whom information is supplied under section 41A may not disclose that information.

(2) But subsection (1) does not apply to a disclosure—

(a) which is made for the purpose of a customs function, where the disclosure does not contravene any restriction imposed by the Commissioners for Her Majesty's Revenue and Customs;

(b) which is made for the purposes of civil proceedings (whether or not within the United Kingdom) relating to a customs function;

(c) which is made for the purpose of a criminal investigation or criminal proceedings (whether or not within the United Kingdom);

(d) which is made in pursuance of an order of a court;

(e) which is made with the consent (which may be general or specific) of HMRC or the RCPO, depending on by whom or on whose behalf the information was supplied;

(f) which is made with the consent of each person to whom the information relates.

(3) Subsection (1) is subject to any other enactment permitting disclosure.

(4) The reference in subsection (1) to information supplied under section 41A includes a reference to documents or articles supplied by virtue of subsection (3) of that section.

(5) The reference in that subsection to a person to whom information is supplied includes a reference to a person who is or was acting on behalf of that person.

(6) In subsection (3) "enactment" does not include—

(a) an Act of the Scottish Parliament,

(b) an Act of the Northern Ireland Assembly, or

(c) an instrument made under an Act within paragraph (a) or (b)."

(2) In section 42(1) of that Act (wrongful disclosure) after "section 41" insert "or 41B".

21 Duty to share information

(1) In section 36 of the Immigration, Asylum and Nationality Act 2006 (c. 13) (duty to share information), in subsection (1), for paragraph (a) substitute—

"(a) designated customs officials,

(aa) immigration officers,

(ab) the Secretary of State in so far as the Secretary of State has general customs functions,

(ac) the Secretary of State in so far as the Secretary of State has functions relating to immigration, asylum or nationality,

(ad) the Director of Border Revenue and any person exercising functions of the Director,".

(2) In subsection (6)(a) of that section, after "persons" insert "or descriptions of persons".

(3) In subsection (9) of that section, at the appropriate place insert—

"“designated customs official” and “general customs function” have the meanings given by Part 1 of the Borders, Citizenship and Immigration Act 2009,”.

Investigations and detention

22 Application of the PACE orders

(1) Subject as follows, the PACE orders—

(a) apply to criminal investigations conducted by designated customs officials and relating to a general customs matter or customs revenue matter as they apply to relevant investigations conducted by officers of Revenue and Customs, and

(b) apply to persons detained by designated customs officials as they apply to persons detained by officers of Revenue and Customs.

(2) Each of the following is a PACE order for the purposes of this section—

(a) the Police and Criminal Evidence Act 1984 (Application to Revenue and Customs) Order 2007 (S.I. 2007/3175);

(b) the Police and Criminal Evidence (Application to Revenue and Customs) Order (Northern Ireland) 2007 (S.R. 2007/464).

(3) In the application of the PACE orders by virtue of this section—

(a) subject to the following provisions of this subsection, references in those orders to an officer of Revenue and Customs are to be read as references to a designated customs official;

(b) references in those orders to the Commissioners are to be read as references to—

(i) the Secretary of State in relation to general customs matters, or

(ii) the Director of Border Revenue in relation to customs revenue matters;

(c) references in those orders to Her Majesty's Revenue and Customs or to Revenue and Customs are to be read as references to—

(i) the Secretary of State in so far as the Secretary of State has general customs functions,

(ii) the Director of Border Revenue, and

(iii) designated customs officials;

(d) references in those orders to an office of Revenue and Customs are to be read as references to an office of the UK Border Agency;

(e) references in those orders to a designated office of Revenue and Customs are to be read as references to a designated office of the UK Border Agency;

(f) references in those orders to a relevant indictable offence are to be read as references to an indictable offence that relates to a general customs matter or a customs revenue matter;

(g) references in those orders to a relevant investigation are to be read as references to a criminal investigation conducted by a designated customs official that relates to a general customs matter or a customs revenue matter;

(h) references in those orders to a person being in Revenue and Customs detention are to be read as references to a person being in UK Border Agency detention;

(i) references in those orders to an officer of Revenue and Customs of at least the grade of officer are to be read as references to a designated customs official of at least the grade of immigration officer or executive officer;

(j) references in those orders to an officer of Revenue and Customs of at least the grade of higher officer are to be read as references to a designated customs official of at least the grade of chief immigration officer or higher executive officer;

(k) references in those orders to an officer of Revenue and Customs of at least the grade of senior officer are to be read as references to a designated customs official of at least the grade of immigration inspector or senior executive officer;

(l) any other references in those orders to an officer of Revenue and Customs occupying a specified post or grade are to be read as references to the Secretary of State.

(4) For the purposes of this section—

(a) a person is in UK Border Agency detention if—

(i) the person has been taken to an office of the UK Border Agency after being arrested for an offence, or

(ii) the person is arrested at an office of the UK Border Agency after attending voluntarily at the office or accompanying a designated customs official to it,

and is detained there or is detained elsewhere in the charge of a designated customs official, and

(b) "office of the UK Border Agency" means premises wholly or partly occupied by designated customs officials.

(5) This section does not apply to the following provisions of the PACE orders—

(a) in article 2(1) of the Police and Criminal Evidence Act 1984 (Application to Revenue and Customs) Order 2007 (S.I. 2007/3175), the definitions of "the Commissioners", "office of Revenue and Customs", "relevant indictable offence" and "relevant investigation";

(b) article 2(2) of that order (Revenue and Customs detention);

(c) article 7 of that order (restriction on other powers to apply for production of documents);

(d) article 19 of that order (authorisation);

(e) in article 2(1) of the Police and Criminal Evidence (Application to Revenue and Customs) Order (Northern Ireland) 2007 (S.R. 2007/464), the definitions of "the Commissioners", "office of Revenue and Customs", "relevant indictable offence" and "relevant investigation";

(f) article 2(2) of that order (Revenue and Customs detention);

(g) article 7 of that order (restriction on other powers to apply for production of documents);

(h) article 15 of that order (authorisation).

(6) A person may be transferred—

(a) between UK Border Agency detention and Revenue and Customs detention;

(b) between Revenue and Customs detention and UK Border Agency detention;

(c) between UK Border Agency detention and police detention;

(d) between police detention and UK Border Agency detention.

(7) The references to police detention in subsection (6)—

(a) in relation to England and Wales, are to be construed in accordance with the Police and Criminal Evidence Act 1984 (c. 60);

(b) in relation to Northern Ireland, are to be construed in accordance with the Police and Criminal Evidence (Northern Ireland) Order 1989 (S.I. 1989/1341 (N.I. 12)).

(8) Expressions used in this section that are defined in a PACE order have the same meaning as in that PACE order.

(9) This section does not affect the generality of sections 1(4), 3(5), 7(5) and 11(4) (construction of statutory etc. references to the Commissioners for Her Majesty's Revenue and Customs, officers of Revenue and Customs and Her Majesty's Revenue and Customs).

23 Investigations and detention: England and Wales and Northern Ireland

(1) The Secretary of State may by order provide for any provision of an enactment listed in subsection (2) that relates to investigations of offences conducted by police officers or to persons detained by the police to apply, subject to such modifications as the order may specify, in relation to—

(a) investigations conducted by designated customs officials,

(b) persons detained by designated customs officials,

(c) investigations conducted by immigration officers, or

(d) persons detained by immigration officers.

(2) Those enactments are—

(a) the Police and Criminal Evidence Act 1984 (c. 60), and

(b) the Police and Criminal Evidence (Northern Ireland) Order 1989 (S.I. 1989/1341 (N.I. 12)).

(3) An order under this section may make, in relation to designated customs officials, immigration officers, the Secretary of State or the Director of Border Revenue, provision similar to that which may be made in relation to officers of Revenue and Customs or the Commissioners for Her Majesty's Revenue and Customs under—

(a) section 114 of the Police and Criminal Evidence Act 1984, or

(b) article 85 of the Police and Criminal Evidence (Northern Ireland) Order 1989.

(4) If an order under this section provides that a function may be exercised only by a person acting with the authority of the Secretary of State or the Director of Border Revenue, a certificate of the Secretary of State or (as the case may be) the Director that the person had authority to exercise the function is conclusive evidence of that fact.

(5) An order under this section may amend or repeal section 22 (application of the PACE orders).

24 Investigations and detention: Scotland

(1) After section 26B of the Criminal Law (Consolidation) (Scotland) Act 1995 (c. 39) insert—

"26C Investigations by designated customs officials

(1) In the application of this Part of this Act to investigations conducted by designated customs officials—

(a) references to an officer are to a designated customs official;

(b) references to an authorised officer are to a designated customs official acting with the authority (which may be general or specific) of—

(i) the Secretary of State in relation to investigations relating to general customs matters, or

(ii) the Director of Border Revenue in relation to investigations relating to customs revenue matters;

(c) references to the Commissioners for Her Majesty's Revenue and Customs are to—

(i) the Secretary of State in relation to investigations relating to general customs matters, or

(ii) the Director of Border Revenue in relation to investigations relating to customs revenue matters;

(d) references to an office of Revenue and Customs are to premises wholly or partly occupied by designated customs officials;

(e) references to a superior officer are to—

(i) an immigration officer not below the grade of Inspector,

(ii) a person of the grade of Senior Executive Officer, or

(iii) a person of a grade equivalent to that within sub-paragraph (i) or (ii).

(2) In this section "customs revenue matter", "designated customs official" and "general customs matter" have the meanings given by Part 1 of the Borders, Citizenship and Immigration Act 2009."

(2) The amendment made by this section does not affect the generality of sections 1(4), 3(5), 7(5) and 11(4) (construction of statutory etc. references to the Commissioners for Her Majesty's Revenue and Customs, officers of Revenue and Customs and Her Majesty's Revenue and Customs).

25 Short-term holding facilities

In section 147 of the Immigration and Asylum Act 1999 (c. 33) (removal centres and detained persons: interpretation), in the definition of "short-term holding facility"—

(a) after "used" insert "—(a)", and

(b) at the end insert ", or

(b) for the detention of—

(i) detained persons for a period of not more than seven days or for such other period as may be prescribed, and

(ii) persons other than detained persons for any period."

Transfer of property etc.

26 Transfer schemes

(1) The Commissioners for Her Majesty's Revenue and Customs may make one or more schemes for the transfer of specified property, rights or liabilities or property, rights or liabilities of a specified description between—

(a) the Commissioners or officers of Revenue and Customs, and

(b) the Secretary of State, the Director of Border Revenue or designated customs officials.

(2) A scheme under subsection (1) may, in particular—

(a) create interests or rights, or impose liabilities, in relation to property, rights or liabilities transferred by virtue of the scheme or retained by a transferor;

(b) apportion property, rights or liabilities between a transferor and a transferee.

(3) A scheme under subsection (1) may—

(a) provide for anything done by or in relation to a transferor in connection with anything transferred to have effect as if done by or in relation to a transferee;

(b) permit anything (including any legal proceedings) relating to anything transferred by the scheme which is in the process of being done by or in relation to a transferor when the transfer takes effect to be continued by or in relation to a transferee;

(c) provide for references to a transferor in an agreement (whether written or not), instrument or other document relating to anything transferred by the scheme to be treated as references to a transferee;

(d) include other incidental, supplementary, consequential, transitional or transitory provision or savings.

(4) A scheme under subsection (1) may provide for a transfer of property, rights or liabilities—

(a) whether or not they would otherwise be capable of being transferred,

(b) without any instrument or other formality being required, and

(c) irrespective of any requirement for consent that would otherwise apply.

(5) The Commissioners may make one or more schemes providing for—

(a) any specified thing or anything of a specified description done by or in relation to the Commissioners or an officer of Revenue and Customs in connection with a relevant function to have effect as if done by or in relation to the Secretary of State, the Director or a designated customs official;

(b) any specified thing or anything of a specified description (including any legal proceedings) relating to a relevant function done by or in relation to the Commissioners or an officer of Revenue and Customs to be continued by or in relation to the Secretary of State, the Director or a designated customs official.

(6) A scheme under this section—

(a) comes into force in accordance with its terms;

(b) may be amended or revoked.

(7) In this section—

"relevant function" means a function which before the passing of this Act was exercisable by the Commissioners or officers of Revenue and Customs (whether or not it remains so exercisable) and that—

(a) is conferred by or by virtue of this Part on the Secretary of State, the Director or a designated customs official, or

(b) is a function under Community law that is exercisable by the Secretary of State, the Director or a designated customs official;

"specified" means specified in the scheme.

27 Facilities and services

(1) Her Majesty's Revenue and Customs may make facilities and services available to any person by whom functions relating to immigration, asylum or nationality, or customs functions, are exercisable for the purposes of the exercise of any of those functions.

(2) A person by whom functions relating to immigration, asylum or nationality, or customs functions, are exercisable may make facilities and services available to Her Majesty's Revenue and Customs for the purposes of the exercise of a function of Her Majesty's Revenue and Customs.

Inspection and oversight

28 Inspections by the Chief Inspector of the UK Border Agency

(1) In section 48 of the UK Borders Act 2007 (c. 30) (establishment of the Border and Immigration Inspectorate), in subsection (1) for "the Border and Immigration Agency" substitute "the UK Border Agency".

(2) After that subsection insert—

"(1A) The Chief Inspector shall monitor and report on the efficiency and effectiveness of the performance of functions by the following—

(a) designated customs officials, and officials of the Secretary of State exercising customs functions;

(b) immigration officers, and officials of the Secretary of State exercising functions relating to immigration, asylum or nationality;

(c) the Secretary of State in so far as the Secretary of State has general customs functions;

(d) the Secretary of State in so far as the Secretary of State has functions relating to immigration, asylum or nationality;

(e) the Director of Border Revenue and any person exercising functions of the Director.

(1B) The Chief Inspector shall monitor and report on the efficiency and effectiveness of the services provided by a person acting pursuant to arrangements relating to the discharge of a function within subsection (1A)."

(3) In subsection (2) of that section—

(a) omit the words from the beginning to "Agency;",

(b) in paragraph (a), for "within the Border and Immigration Agency" substitute "among the persons listed in subsections (1A) and (1B) (the "listed persons")",

(c) in paragraph (b), for "the Border and Immigration Agency" substitute "the listed persons", and

(d) after paragraph (g) insert—

"(ga) practice and procedure in relation to the prevention, detection and investigation of offences,

(gb) practice and procedure in relation to the conduct of criminal proceedings,

(gc) whether customs functions have been appropriately exercised by the Secretary of State and the Director of Border Revenue,".

(4) After that subsection insert—

"(2A) Unless directed to do so by the Secretary of State, the Chief Inspector shall not monitor and report on the exercise by the listed persons of—

(a) functions at removal centres and short term holding facilities, and under escort arrangements, in so far as Her Majesty's Chief Inspector of Prisons has functions under section 5A of the Prison Act 1952 in relation to such functions, and

(b) functions at detention facilities, in so far as Her Majesty's Inspectors of Constabulary, the Scottish inspectors or the Northern Ireland inspectors have functions by virtue of section 29 of the Borders, Citizenship and Immigration Act 2009 in relation to such functions."

(5) Omit subsection (3) of that section.

(6) After that subsection insert—

"(3A) In this section "customs function", "designated customs official" and "general customs function" have the meanings given by Part 1 of the Borders, Citizenship and Immigration Act 2009."

(7) In section 53 of that Act (relationship with other bodies), in subsection (1)—

(a) in paragraph (a), for "the Border and Immigration Agency" substitute "a person listed in section 48(1A) or (1B)", and

(b) in paragraph (b), for "the Agency" substitute "such a person".

(8) In subsection (3) of that section, for "the Agency" insert "a person listed in section 48(1A) or (1B)".

(9) In section 56(2)(a) of that Act (Senior President of Tribunals), for "the Border and Immigration Agency" substitute "the UK Border Agency".

(10) The person holding the office of the Chief Inspector of the Border and Immigration Agency immediately before the day on which this section comes into force is to be treated, on and after that day, as if appointed as the Chief Inspector of the UK Border Agency under section 48(1) of the UK Borders Act 2007 (c. 30).

29 Inspections by Her Majesty's Inspectors of Constabulary etc.

(1) The Secretary of State may make regulations conferring functions on Her Majesty's Inspectors of Constabulary, the Scottish inspectors or the Northern Ireland inspectors in relation to—

(a) designated customs officials, and officials of the Secretary of State exercising customs functions;

(b) immigration officers, and officials of the Secretary of State exercising functions relating to immigration, asylum or nationality;

(c) the Secretary of State in so far as the Secretary of State has general customs functions;

(d) the Secretary of State in so far as the Secretary of State has functions relating to immigration, asylum or nationality;

(e) the Director of Border Revenue and any person exercising functions of the Director;

(f) persons providing services pursuant to arrangements relating to the discharge of a function of a person mentioned in paragraphs (a) to (e).

(2) Regulations under subsection (1) may—

(a) in relation to Her Majesty's Inspectors of Constabulary, apply (with or without modification) or make provision similar to any provision of sections 54 to 56 of the Police Act 1996 (c. 16) (inspection);

(b) in relation to the Scottish inspectors, apply (with or without modification) or make provision similar to any provision of section 33 or 34 of the Police (Scotland) Act 1967 (c. 77) (inspection);

(c) in relation to the Northern Ireland inspectors, apply (without or without modification) or make provision similar to any provision of section 41 or 42 of the Police (Northern Ireland) Act 1998 (c. 32) (inspection).

(3) Regulations under subsection (1)—

(a) may enable a Minister of the Crown to require an inspection to be carried out;

(b) must provide for a report of an inspection to be made and, subject to any exceptions required or permitted by the regulations, published;

(c) must provide for an annual report by Her Majesty's Inspectors of Constabulary;

(d) may make provision for payment to or in respect of Her Majesty's Inspectors of Constabulary, the Scottish inspectors or the Northern Ireland inspectors.

(4) An inspection carried out by virtue of this section may not address a matter of a kind which the Comptroller and Auditor General may examine under section 6 of the National Audit Act 1983 (c. 44).

(5) An inspection carried out by virtue of this section must be carried out jointly by Her Majesty's Inspectors of Constabulary and the Scottish inspectors—

(a) if it is carried out wholly in Scotland, or

(b) in a case where it is carried out partly in Scotland, to the extent that it is carried out there.

(6) In this section—

(a) "the Scottish inspectors" means the inspectors of constabulary appointed under section 33(1) of the Police (Scotland) Act 1967;

(b) "the Northern Ireland inspectors" means the inspectors of constabulary appointed under section 41(1) of the Police (Northern Ireland) Act 1998.

30 Complaints and misconduct

(1) In section 41 of the Police and Justice Act 2006 (c. 48) (power to confer functions on the Independent Police Complaints Commission in respect of the exercise of immigration functions)—

(a) after subsection (1)(b) insert—

"(c) the provision of services pursuant to arrangements relating to the discharge of a function within paragraph (a) or (b).", and

(b) after subsection (2) insert—

"(2A) The Secretary of State may make regulations conferring functions on the Independent Police Complaints Commission in relation to—

(a) the exercise by designated customs officials, and officials of the Secretary of State, of customs functions within the meaning of Part 1 of the Borders, Citizenship and Immigration Act 2009;

(b) the exercise by the Director of Border Revenue, and any person exercising functions of the Director, of customs revenue functions within the meaning of that Part of that Act;

(c) the provision of services pursuant to arrangements relating to the discharge of a function within paragraph (a) or (b)."

(2) In each of subsections (4) and (7) of that section, after "subsection (1)" insert "or (2A)".

(3) In the title to that section, after "functions" insert "and customs functions".

Other provisions

31 Prosecution of offences

(1) The Attorney General may by order assign to the Director of Revenue and Customs Prosecutions a function of—

(a) instituting criminal proceedings in England and Wales,

(b) assuming the conduct of criminal proceedings in England and Wales, or

(c) providing legal advice,

relating to a criminal investigation of a kind specified in the order by a person to whom this section applies.

(2) This section applies to—

(a) designated customs officials,

(b) immigration officers,

(c) officials of the Secretary of State,

(d) the Secretary of State,

(e) the Director of Border Revenue,

(f) a person acting on behalf of a person mentioned in paragraphs (a) to (e), and

(g) constables.

(3) For the purposes of the Commissioners for Revenue and Customs Act 2005 (c. 11)—

(a) functions assigned to the Director of Revenue and Customs Prosecutions by virtue of this section are to be treated as functions of the Director under or by virtue of that Act, and
(b) proceedings conducted by the Director by virtue of this section are to be treated as proceedings conducted by the Director under that Act.

(4) Sections 37 to 37B of the Police and Criminal Evidence Act 1984 (c. 60) (guidance etc.) have effect, in relation to a person arrested following a criminal investigation in relation to which functions are conferred by virtue of this section, as if references to the Director of Public Prosecutions were references to the Director of Revenue and Customs Prosecutions.

(5) An order under this section—
(a) may include incidental, supplementary and consequential provision;
(b) may make transitional or transitory provision or savings;
(c) may be amended or revoked.

(6) The reference in this section to instituting criminal proceedings is to be construed in accordance with section 15(2) of the Prosecution of Offences Act 1985 (c. 23).

(7) In this section "criminal investigation" means any process—
(a) for considering whether an offence has been committed,
(b) for discovering by whom an offence has been committed, or
(c) as a result of which an offence is alleged to have been committed.

32 Payment of revenue to the Commissioners

(1) The Director of Border Revenue must pay money received by way of revenue or security for revenue in the exercise of the Director's customs revenue functions to the Commissioners for Her Majesty's Revenue and Customs.

(2) The Secretary of State must pay money received by way of revenue in the exercise of the Secretary of State's general customs functions to the Commissioners.

(3) A payment under subsection (1) or (2) must be made—
(a) at such times and in such manner as the Treasury directs, and
(b) after deduction of payments in connection with drawback and repayments.

(4) If the Commissioners think that the funds available to the Director or the Secretary of State may be insufficient to make a payment in connection with drawback or a repayment, the Commissioners may—
(a) pay money to the Director or the Secretary of State (as the case may be) to enable the payment or repayment to be made, or
(b) make the payment or repayment on behalf of the Director or the Secretary of State (as the case may be).

(5) Subsection (4) applies whether or not the reason for a deficiency is or may be that an amount has been paid or retained on the basis of an estimate that has proved or may prove to be inaccurate.

(6) A payment by the Commissioners under that subsection is to be treated for the purposes of the Commissioners for Revenue and Customs Act 2005 (c. 11) as a disbursement of a kind specified in section 44(3) of that Act.

(7) In this section—

"repayments" includes—

(a) payments in respect of actual or deemed credits relating to any tax, duty or levy, and

(b) payments of interest (or repayment supplement) on—

(i) repayments, or

(ii) payments treated as repayments;

"revenue" means—

(a) taxes, duties and levies,

(b) the proceeds of forfeitures made and penalties imposed under the customs and excise Acts (within the meaning of section 1 of the Customs and Excise Management Act 1979 (c. 2)),

(c) a sum paid, or the proceeds of sale, under paragraph 16 of Schedule 3 to that Act, and

(d) the proceeds of penalties imposed in accordance with Regulation (EC) No 1889/2005 on controls of cash entering or leaving the Community (including penalties imposed under that Regulation as amended from time to time);

"security for revenue" means any sum paid as security for a tax or duty.

33 Power to require payment into the Consolidated Fund

(1) The Treasury may by order make provision for—

(a) requiring the payment of sums received by the Secretary of State or the Director in the exercise of their functions into the Consolidated Fund;

(b) permitting the deduction of disbursements before such payments are made;

(c) requiring the Secretary of State or the Director to provide accounts of the receipt and disposal of revenue;

(d) permitting the Treasury to make payments to the Secretary of State or the Director out of the Consolidated Fund to enable them to make disbursements.

(2) An order under this section may amend or repeal section 32 (payment of revenue to the Commissioners).

34 Children

(1) In section 21 of the UK Borders Act 2007 (c. 30) (code of practice relating to children), in subsection (1), for "the Border and Immigration Agency takes" substitute "the persons listed in subsection (4A) take".

(2) In subsection (2) of that section—

(a) for "The Agency" substitute "Those persons",

(b) in paragraph (a), for "its" substitute "their", and

(c) in paragraph (b), for "it makes" substitute "they make".

(3) After subsection (4) of that section insert—

"(4A) The persons are—

(a) designated customs officials, and officials of the Secretary of State exercising customs functions,

(b) immigration officers, and officials of the Secretary of State exercising functions relating to immigration, asylum or nationality,

(c) the Secretary of State in so far as the Secretary of State has general customs functions,

(d) the Secretary of State in so far as the Secretary of State has functions relating to immigration, asylum or nationality, and

(e) the Director of Border Revenue and any person exercising functions of the Director."

(4) In subsection (5) of that section omit paragraph (a).

(5) After that subsection insert—

"(5A) In this section "customs function", "designated customs official" and "general customs function" have the meanings given by Part 1 of the Borders, Citizenship and Immigration Act 2009."

(6) This section ceases to have effect on the coming into force of section 55 (duty regarding welfare of children).

Supplementary

35 Power to modify enactments

(1) The Secretary of State may by order provide for an enactment (or a description of enactments) to apply in relation to—

(a) relevant persons, or

(b) the exercise of functions by relevant persons,

with such modifications as the Secretary of State considers necessary or expedient.

(2) In this section—

(a) "relevant persons" means—

(i) the Secretary of State by whom general customs functions are exercisable,

(ii) the Director of Border Revenue, and

(iii) designated customs officials, immigration officers and officials in the department of that Secretary of State, and

(b) a reference to relevant persons includes a reference to any description of relevant persons.

(3) An order under this section may, in particular, include provision for or in connection with—

(a) extending to relevant persons an exemption or protection afforded by an enactment to any other description of persons;

(b) providing for the disclosure of information to, or the doing of other things in relation to, relevant persons.

(4) The Secretary of State must consult the Commissioners for Her Majesty's Revenue and Customs before making an order under this section that—

(a) makes provision in relation to a general customs matter or a customs revenue matter, or

(b) makes provision in relation to the exercise of a customs function.

36 Power to make supplementary etc. provision

(1) The Secretary of State may by order make—

(a) such incidental, supplementary or consequential provision, or

(b) such transitional or transitory provision or savings,

as the Secretary of State considers appropriate for the general purposes, or any particular purpose, of this Part, or in consequence of, or for giving full effect to, any provision made by or under this Part.

(2) An order under subsection (1) may amend, repeal, revoke or otherwise modify any enactment (including this Act).

(3) The power to make an order under subsection (1) includes power to repeal or revoke an enactment which is spent.

(4) Nothing in this Part affects the generality of the power conferred by this section.

37 Subordinate legislation

(1) Orders and regulations under this Part must be made by statutory instrument.

(2) An order or regulations under this Part may—

(a) include incidental, supplementary and consequential provision;

(b) make transitional or transitory provision or savings;

(c) make different provision for different cases or circumstances.

(3) A statutory instrument containing an order or regulations to which subsection (4) applies may not be made unless a draft of the instrument has been laid before, and approved by a resolution of, each House of Parliament.

(4) This subsection applies to—

(a) an order under section 2 (power of Secretary of State to modify functions);

(b) an order under section 8 (power of Treasury to modify Director's functions);

(c) regulations under section 16(8) (power to permit disclosure);

(d) an order under section 23 (application of provisions about investigations and detention: England and Wales and Northern Ireland);

(e) an order under section 35 (power to modify enactments);

(f) an order under section 36 (power to make supplementary etc. provision) that amends or repeals primary legislation.

(5) A statutory instrument containing only—

(a) regulations under section 29 (inspections by Her Majesty's Inspectors of Constabulary etc.), or

(b) an order under section 36 that does not amend or repeal primary legislation,

is subject to annulment in pursuance of a resolution of either House of Parliament.

(6) A statutory instrument containing an order under section 33 (power to require payment into the Consolidated Fund) is subject to annulment in pursuance of a resolution of the House of Commons.

(7) In this section "primary legislation" means—

(a) an Act of Parliament,

(b) an Act of the Scottish Parliament,

(c) a Measure or Act of the National Assembly for Wales, or

(d) Northern Ireland legislation.

(8) This section does not apply to an order under section 31 (prosecution of offences).

38 Interpretation

In this Part—

"Community law" means—

(a) all the rights, powers, liabilities, obligations and restrictions from time to time created or arising by or under the Community Treaties, and

(b) all the remedies and procedures from time to time provided for by or under the Community Treaties,

as in accordance with the Community Treaties are without further enactment to be given legal effect or used in the United Kingdom;

"customs function" has the meaning given by section 14(6);

"customs information" has the meaning given by section 14(6);

"customs revenue function" has the meaning given by section 7(9);

"customs revenue information" has the meaning given by section 14(6);

"customs revenue matter" has the meaning given by section 7(2);

"customs revenue official" means a customs revenue official designated under section 11(1);

"designated customs official" has the meaning given by section 14(6);

"enactment" includes—

(a) an enactment contained in subordinate legislation within the meaning of the Interpretation Act 1978 (c. 30);

(b) an enactment contained in, or in an instrument made under, an Act of the Scottish Parliament;

(c) an enactment contained in, or in instrument made under, Northern Ireland legislation;

(d) an enactment contained in, or in an instrument made under, a Measure or Act of the National Assembly for Wales;

"function" means any power or duty (including a power or duty that is ancillary to another power or duty);

"general customs function" has the meaning given by section 1(8);

"general customs matter" has the meaning given by section 1(2);

"general customs official" means a general customs official designated under section 3(1);

"personal customs information" has the meaning given by section 15(4);

"personal customs revenue information" has the meaning given by section 15(4);

"relevant official" has the meaning given by section 15(3).

PART 2

CITIZENSHIP

Acquisition of British citizenship by naturalisation

39 Application requirements: general

(1) In paragraph 1 of Schedule 1 to the British Nationality Act 1981 (c. 61) (requirements for naturalisation as a British citizen under section 6(1) of that Act), in sub-paragraph (1)(a), omit ", or the alternative requirement specified in sub-paragraph (3) of this paragraph".

(2) For sub-paragraph (2) of that paragraph substitute—

"(2) The requirements referred to in sub-paragraph (1)(a) of this paragraph are—

(a) that the applicant ("A") was in the United Kingdom at the beginning of the qualifying period;

(b) that the number of days on which A was absent from the United Kingdom in each year of the qualifying period does not exceed 90;

(c) that A had a qualifying immigration status for the whole of the qualifying period;

(d) that on the date of the application A has probationary citizenship leave, permanent residence leave, a qualifying CTA entitlement, a Commonwealth right of abode or a permanent EEA entitlement;

(e) that, where on the date of the application A has probationary citizenship leave granted for the purpose of taking employment in the United Kingdom, A has been in continuous employment since the date of the grant of that leave; and

(f) that A was not at any time in the qualifying period in the United Kingdom in breach of the immigration laws."

(3) Omit sub-paragraph (3) of that paragraph.

(4) In paragraph 2 of that Schedule (which becomes sub-paragraph (1) of that paragraph) (discretion of Secretary of State on applications for naturalisation under section 6(1)), for paragraph (a) substitute—

"(a) treat the applicant as fulfilling the requirement specified in paragraph 1(2)(b) although the number of days on which the applicant was absent from the United Kingdom in a year of the qualifying period exceeds 90;".

(5) After paragraph (b) of sub-paragraph (1) of that paragraph, insert—

"(ba) treat the applicant as fulfilling the requirement specified in paragraph 1(2)(c) where the applicant has had a qualifying immigration status for only part of the qualifying period;

(bb) treat the applicant as fulfilling the requirement specified in paragraph 1(2)(d) where the applicant has had probationary citizenship leave but it expired in the qualifying period;".

(6) Omit paragraph (c) of that sub-paragraph.

(7) Before paragraph (d) of that sub-paragraph, insert—

"(ca) treat the applicant as fulfilling the requirement specified in paragraph 1(2)(e) although the applicant has not been in continuous employment since the date of the grant mentioned there;".

(8) In paragraph (d) of that sub-paragraph—

(a) for "1(2)(d)" substitute "1(2)(f)", and

(b) for "period there mentioned" substitute "qualifying period".

(9) After that sub-paragraph insert—

"(2) If in the special circumstances of a particular case that is an armed forces case or an exceptional Crown service case the Secretary of State thinks fit, the Secretary of State may for the purposes of paragraph 1 waive the need to fulfil all or any of the requirements specified in paragraph 1(2).

(3) An armed forces case is a case where, on the date of the application, the applicant is or has been a member of the armed forces.

(4) An exceptional Crown service case is a case where—

(a) the applicant is, on the date of the application, serving outside the United Kingdom in Crown service under the government of the United Kingdom; and

(b) the Secretary of State considers the applicant's performance in the service to be exceptional."

(10) After sub-paragraph (4) (inserted by subsection (9) above) insert—

"(5) In paragraph 1(2)(e) and sub-paragraph (1)(ca) of this paragraph, "employment" includes self-employment."

(11) After paragraph 2 insert—

"2A (1) A person has a qualifying immigration status for the purposes of paragraph 1(2) if the person has—

(a) qualifying temporary residence leave;

(b) probationary citizenship leave;

(c) permanent residence leave;

(d) a qualifying CTA entitlement;

(e) a Commonwealth right of abode; or

(f) a temporary or permanent EEA entitlement.

(2) A person who is required for those purposes to have a qualifying immigration status for the whole of the qualifying period need not have the same qualifying immigration status for the whole of that period."

40 Application requirements: family members etc.

(1) In section 6 of the British Nationality Act 1981 (c. 61) (acquisition of British citizenship by naturalisation), in subsection (2), for "is married to a British citizen or is the civil partner of a British citizen" substitute "has a relevant family association".

(2) After that subsection insert—

"(3) For the purposes of this section and Schedule 1, a person ("A") has a relevant family association if A has a connection of a prescribed description to a person of a prescribed description.

(4) If in the special circumstances of any particular case the Secretary of State thinks fit, the Secretary of State may for the purposes of subsection (3) treat A as having a relevant family association on the date of the application although the relevant family association ceased to exist before that date."

(3) For paragraph 3 of Schedule 1 to that Act (requirements for naturalisation as a British citizen under section 6(2) of that Act) substitute—

"3 (1) Subject to paragraph 4, the requirements for naturalisation as a British citizen under section 6(2) are, in the case of any person ("A") who applies for it—

(a) the requirements specified in sub-paragraph (2) of this paragraph;

(b) the requirement specified in sub-paragraph (3) of this paragraph;

(c) that A is of good character;

(d) that A has a sufficient knowledge of the English, Welsh or Scottish Gaelic language; and

(e) that A has sufficient knowledge about life in the United Kingdom.

(2) The requirements referred to in sub-paragraph (1)(a) are—

(a) that A was in the United Kingdom at the beginning of the qualifying period;

(b) that the number of days on which A was absent from the United Kingdom in each year of the qualifying period does not exceed 90;

(c) that, subject to sub-paragraph (5)—

(i) A had a relevant family association for the whole of the qualifying period, and

(ii) A had a qualifying immigration status for the whole of that period;

(d) that on the date of the application—

(i) A has probationary citizenship leave, or permanent residence leave, based on A's having the relevant family association referred to in section 6(2), or

(ii) A has a qualifying CTA entitlement or a Commonwealth right of abode; and

(e) that A was not at any time in the qualifying period in the United Kingdom in breach of the immigration laws.

(3) The requirement referred to in sub-paragraph (1)(b) is—

(a) that A's intentions are such that, in the event of a certificate of naturalisation as a British citizen being granted to A, A's home or (if A has more than one) A's principal home will be in the United Kingdom;

(b) that A intends, in the event of such a certificate being granted to A, to enter into, or continue in, service of a description mentioned in sub-paragraph (4); or

(c) that, in the event of such a certificate being granted to A—

(i) the person with whom A has the relevant family association referred to in section 6(2) ("B") intends to enter into, or continue in, service of a description mentioned in sub-paragraph (4); and

(ii) A intends to reside with B for the period during which B is in the service in question.

(4) The descriptions of service referred to in sub-paragraph (3) are—

(a) Crown service under the government of the United Kingdom;

(b) service under an international organisation of which the United Kingdom, or Her Majesty's government in the United Kingdom, is a member; or

(c) service in the employment of a company or association established in the United Kingdom.

(5) Where the relevant family association referred to in section 6(2) is (in accordance with regulations under section 41(1)(a)) that A is the partner of a person who is a British citizen or who has permanent residence leave—

(a) the requirement specified in sub-paragraph (2)(c)(i) is fulfilled only if A was that person's partner for the whole of the qualifying period, and

(b) for the purposes of sub-paragraph (2)(c)(ii), A can rely upon having a qualifying immigration status falling within paragraph 4A(1)(a), (b) or (c) only if that partnership is the relevant family association upon which the leave to which the status relates is based.

(6) For the purposes of sub-paragraph (5), A is a person's partner if—

(a) that person is A's spouse or civil partner or is in a relationship with A that is of a description that the regulations referred to in that sub-paragraph specify, and

(b) the marriage, civil partnership or other relationship satisfies the conditions (if any) that those regulations specify.

(7) For the purposes of sub-paragraph (5), the relationship by reference to which A and the other person are partners need not be of the same description for the whole of the qualifying period."

(4) For paragraph 4 of that Schedule substitute—

"4 If in the special circumstances of any particular case the Secretary of State thinks fit, the Secretary of State may for the purposes of paragraph 3 do all or any of the following, namely—

(a) treat A as fulfilling the requirement specified in paragraph 3(2)(b), although the number of days on which A was absent from the United Kingdom in a year of the qualifying period exceeds 90;

(b) treat A as having been in the United Kingdom for the whole or any part of any period during which A would otherwise fall to be treated under paragraph 9(1) as having been absent;

(c) treat A as fulfilling the requirement specified in paragraph 3(2)(c)(i) (including where it can be fulfilled only as set out in paragraph 3(5)) where a relevant family association of A's has ceased to exist;

(d) treat A as fulfilling the requirement specified in paragraph 3(2)(c)(ii) (including where it can be fulfilled only as set out in paragraph 3(5)) where A has had a qualifying immigration status for only part of the qualifying period;

(e) treat A as fulfilling the requirement specified in paragraph 3(2)(d) where A has had probationary citizenship leave but it expired in the qualifying period;

(f) treat A as fulfilling the requirement specified in paragraph 3(2)(e) although A was in the United Kingdom in breach of the immigration laws in the qualifying period;

(g) waive the need to fulfil either or both of the requirements specified in paragraph 3(1)(d) and (e) if the Secretary of State considers that because of A's age or physical or mental condition it would be unreasonable to expect A to fulfil that requirement or those requirements;

(h) waive the need to fulfil all or any of the requirements specified in paragraph 3(2)(a), (b), (c) or (d) (including where paragraph 3(2)(c) can be fulfilled only as set out in paragraph 3(5)) if—

(i) on the date of the application, the person with whom A has the relevant family association referred to in section 6(2) is serving in service to which section 2(1)(b) applies, and

(ii) that person's recruitment for that service took place in the United Kingdom."

(5) After that paragraph insert—

"4A (1) Subject to paragraph 3(5), a person has a qualifying immigration status for the purposes of paragraph 3 if the person has—

(a) qualifying temporary residence leave based on a relevant family association;

(b) probationary citizenship leave based on a relevant family association;

(c) permanent residence leave based on a relevant family association;

(d) a qualifying CTA entitlement; or

(e) a Commonwealth right of abode.

(2) For the purposes of paragraph 3 and this paragraph, the leave mentioned in sub-paragraph (1)(a), (b) or (c) is based on a relevant family association if it was granted on the basis of the person having a relevant family association.

(3) A person who is required for the purposes of paragraph 3 to have, for the whole of the qualifying period, a qualifying immigration status and a relevant family association need not, for the whole of that period—

(a) have the same qualifying immigration status; or

(b) (subject to paragraph 3(5)) have the same relevant family association.

(4) Where, by virtue of sub-paragraph (3)(a), a person relies upon having more than one qualifying immigration status falling within sub-paragraph (1)(a), (b) or (c)—

(a) subject to paragraph 3(5), it is not necessary that the leave to which each status relates is based on the same relevant family association, and

(b) in a case where paragraph 3(5) applies, the relationship by reference to which the persons referred to in paragraph 3(5) are partners need not be of the same description in respect of each grant of leave."

41 The qualifying period

(1) After paragraph 4A of Schedule 1 to the British Nationality Act 1981 (c. 61) (inserted by section 40(5) above), insert—

"4B The qualifying period for naturalisation as a British citizen under section 6

4B (1) The qualifying period for the purposes of paragraph 1 or 3 is a period of years which ends with the date of the application in question.

(2) The length of the period is determined in accordance with the following provisions of this paragraph.

(3) In the case of an applicant who does not meet the activity condition, the number of years in the period is—

(a) 8, in a case within paragraph 1;

(b) 5, in a case within paragraph 3.

(4) In the case of an applicant who meets the activity condition, the number of years in the period is—

(a) 6, in a case within paragraph 1;

(b) 3, in a case within paragraph 3.

(5) The applicant meets the activity condition if the Secretary of State is satisfied that the applicant—

(a) has participated otherwise than for payment in prescribed activities; or

(b) is to be treated as having so participated."

(2) In section 41 of that Act (regulations etc.), in subsection (1), after paragraph (bb) insert—

"(bc) for amending paragraph 4B(3)(a) or (b) or (4)(a) or (b) of Schedule 1 to substitute a different number for the number for the time being specified there;

(bd) for determining whether a person has, for the purposes of an application for naturalisation under section 6, participated in activities prescribed for the purposes of paragraph 4B(5)(a) of Schedule 1;

(be) for determining whether a person is to be treated for the purposes of such an application as having so participated;".

(3) After subsection (1A) of that section insert—

"(1B) Regulations under subsection (1)(bc) may make provision so that—

(a) the number specified in sub-paragraph (3)(a) of paragraph 4B of Schedule 1 is the same as the number specified in sub-paragraph (4)(a) of that paragraph;

(b) the number specified in sub-paragraph (3)(b) of that paragraph is the same as the number specified in sub-paragraph (4)(b) of that paragraph.

(1C) Regulations under subsection (1)(bd) or (be)—

(a) may make provision that applies in relation to time before the commencement of section 41 of the Borders, Citizenship and Immigration Act 2009;

(b) may enable the Secretary of State to make arrangements for such persons as the Secretary of State thinks appropriate to determine whether, in accordance with those regulations, a person has, or (as the case may be) is to be treated as having, participated in an activity."

(4) In subsection (7) of that section, after "this section" insert "(other than regulations referred to in subsection (8))".

(5) After subsection (7) of that section insert—

"(8) Any regulations (whether alone or with other provision)—

(a) under subsection (1)(a) for prescribing activities for the purposes of paragraph 4B(5)(a) of Schedule 1; or

(b) under subsection (1)(bc), (bd) or (be),

may not be made unless a draft has been laid before and approved by a resolution of each House of Parliament."

Acquisition of British citizenship by birth

42 Children born in UK etc. to members of the armed forces

(1) Section 1 of the British Nationality Act 1981 (c. 61) (acquisition of British citizenship by birth or adoption) is amended as follows.

(2) After subsection (1) insert—

"(1A) A person born in the United Kingdom or a qualifying territory on or after the relevant day shall be a British citizen if at the time of the birth his father or mother is a member of the armed forces."

(3) In subsection (3), after "subsection (1)" insert ", (1A)".

(4) After subsection (3) insert—

"(3A) A person born in the United Kingdom on or after the relevant day who is not a British citizen by virtue of subsection (1), (1A) or (2) shall be entitled to be registered as a British citizen if, while he is a minor—

(a) his father or mother becomes a member of the armed forces; and

(b) an application is made for his registration as a British citizen".

(5) In subsection (4), after "subsection (1)" insert ", (1A)".

(6) After subsection (8) insert—

"(9) The relevant day for the purposes of subsection (1A) or (3A) is the day appointed for the commencement of section 42 of the Borders, Citizenship and Immigration Act 2009 (which inserted those subsections)."

Acquisition of British citizenship etc. by registration

43 Minors

(1) Section 3 of the British Nationality Act 1981 (c. 61) (acquisition by registration: minors) is amended as follows.

(2) In subsection (2), for "within the period of twelve months from the date of the birth" substitute "while he is a minor".

(3) Omit subsection (4).

44 British Nationals (Overseas) without other citizenship

(1) Section 4B of the British Nationality Act 1981 (acquisition by registration: certain persons without other citizenship) is amended as follows.

(2) In subsection (1)—

(a) omit "or" immediately before paragraph (c), and

(b) after that paragraph insert ", or

(d) British National (Overseas)".

(3) In subsection (2)(c), for "4th July 2002" substitute "the relevant day".

(4) After subsection (2), insert—

"(3) For the purposes of subsection (2)(c), the "relevant day" means—

(a) in the case of a person to whom this section applies by virtue of subsection (1)(d) only, 19th March 2009, and

(b) in any other case, 4th July 2002."

45 Descent through the female line

(1) Section 4C of the British Nationality Act 1981 (the title to which becomes "Acquisition by registration: certain persons born before 1983") is amended as follows.

(2) In subsection (2), omit "after 7th February 1961 and".

(3) For subsection (3) substitute—

"(3) The second condition is that the applicant would at some time before 1st January 1983 have become a citizen of the United Kingdom and Colonies—

(a) under section 5 of, or paragraph 3 of Schedule 3 to, the 1948 Act if assumption A had applied,

(b) under section 12(3), (4) or (5) of that Act if assumption B had applied and as a result of its application the applicant would have been a British subject immediately before 1st January 1949, or

(c) under section 12(2) of that Act if one or both of the following had applied—

(i) assumption A had applied;

(ii) assumption B had applied and as a result of its application the applicant would have been a British subject immediately before 1st January 1949.

(3A) Assumption A is that—

(a) section 5 or 12(2) of, or paragraph 3 of Schedule 3 to, the 1948 Act (as the case may be) provided for citizenship by descent from a mother in the same terms as it provided for citizenship by descent from a father, and

(b) references in that provision to a father were references to the applicant's mother.

(3B) Assumption B is that—

(a) a provision of the law at some time before 1st January 1949 which provided for a nationality status to be acquired by descent from a father provided in the same terms for its acquisition by descent from a mother, and

(b) references in that provision to a father were references to the applicant's mother.

(3C) For the purposes of subsection (3B), a nationality status is acquired by a person ("P") by descent where its acquisition—

(a) depends, amongst other things, on the nationality status of one or both of P's parents, and

(b) does not depend upon an application being made for P's registration as a person who has the status in question.

(3D) For the purposes of subsection (3), it is not to be assumed that any registration or other requirements of the provisions mentioned in that subsection or in subsection (3B) were met."

(4) After subsection (4) insert—

"(5) For the purposes of the interpretation of section 5 of the 1948 Act in its application in the case of assumption A to a case of descent from a mother, the reference in the proviso to subsection (1) of that section to "a citizen of the United Kingdom and Colonies by descent only" includes a reference to a female person who became a citizen of the United Kingdom and Colonies by virtue of—

(a) section 12(2), (4) or (6) only of the 1948 Act,

(b) section 13(2) of that Act,

(c) paragraph 3 of Schedule 3 to that Act, or

(d) section 1(1)(a) or (c) of the British Nationality (No. 2) Act 1964."

46 Children born outside UK etc. to members of the armed forces

After section 4C of the British Nationality Act 1981 (c. 61) insert—

"4D Acquisition by registration: children of members of the armed forces

(1) A person ("P") born outside the United Kingdom and the qualifying territories on or after the relevant day is entitled to be registered as a British citizen if—

(a) an application is made for P's registration under this section; and

(b) each of the following conditions is satisfied.

(2) The first condition is that, at the time of P's birth, P's father or mother was—

(a) a member of the armed forces; and

(b) serving outside the United Kingdom and the qualifying territories.

(3) The second condition is that, if P is a minor on the date of the application, the consent of P's father and mother to P's registration as a British citizen has been signified in the prescribed manner.

(4) But if P's father or mother has died on or before the date of the application, the reference in subsection (3) to P's father and mother is to be read as a reference to either of them.

(5) The Secretary of State may, in the special circumstances of a particular case, waive the need for the second condition to be satisfied.

(6) The relevant day for the purposes of this section is the day appointed for the commencement of section 46 of the Borders, Citizenship and Immigration Act 2009 (which inserted this section)."

47 Good character requirement

(1) After section 41 of the British Nationality Act 1981 insert—

"41A Registration: requirement to be of good character

(1) An application for registration of an adult or young person as a British citizen under section 1(3), (3A) or (4), 3(1), (2) or (5), 4(2) or (5), 4A, 4C, 4D, 5, 10(1) or (2) or 13(1) or (3) must not be granted unless the Secretary of State is satisfied that the adult or young person is of good character.

(2) An application for registration of an adult or young person as a British overseas territories citizen under section 15(3) or (4), 17(1) or (5), 22(1) or (2) or 24 must not be granted unless the Secretary of State is satisfied that the adult or young person is of good character.

(3) An application for registration of an adult or young person as a British Overseas citizen under section 27(1) must not be granted unless the Secretary of State is satisfied that the adult or young person is of good character.

(4) An application for registration of an adult or young person as a British subject under section 32 must not be granted unless the Secretary of State is satisfied that the adult or young person is of good character.

(5) In this section, "adult or young person" means a person who has attained the age of 10 years at the time when the application is made."

(2) In section 1 of the Hong Kong (War Wives and Widows) Act 1996 (c. 41) (acquisition of British citizenship), in subsection (1)—

(a) omit "and" immediately before paragraph (b), and

(b) after that paragraph insert "; and

(c) the Secretary of State is satisfied that she is of good character".

(3) In section 1 of the British Nationality (Hong Kong) Act 1997 (c. 20) (acquisition of British citizenship), after subsection (5) insert—

"(5A) An adult or young person shall not be registered under subsection (1) unless the Secretary of State is satisfied that the adult or young person is of good character.

(5B) In subsection (5A), "adult or young person" means a person who has attained the age of 10 years at the time when the application for registration is made."

(4) In section 131 of the Nationality, Immigration and Asylum Act 2002 (c. 41) (supply of police information), for paragraph (b) substitute—

"(b) determining whether, for the purposes of an application referred to in section 41A of the British Nationality Act 1981, the person for whose registration the application is made is of good character;

(ba) determining whether, for the purposes of an application under section 1 of the Hong Kong (War Wives and Widows) Act 1996, the woman for whose registration the application is made is of good character;

(bb) determining whether, for the purposes of an application under section 1 of the British Nationality (Hong Kong) Act 1997 for the registration of an adult or young person within the meaning of subsection (5A) of that section, the person is of good character;".

(5) In section 40 of the UK Borders Act 2007 (c. 30) (supply of Revenue and Customs information), in subsection (1), for paragraph (h) substitute—

"(h) determining whether, for the purposes of an application referred to in section 41A of the British Nationality Act 1981, the person for whose registration the application is made is of good character;

(ha) determining whether, for the purposes of an application under section 1 of the Hong Kong (War Wives and Widows) Act 1996, the woman for whose registration the application is made is of good character;

(hb) determining whether, for the purposes of an application under section 1 of the British Nationality (Hong Kong) Act 1997 for the registration of an adult or young person within the meaning of subsection (5A) of that section, the person is of good character;".

Interpretation etc.

48 Meaning of references to being in breach of immigration laws

(1) After section 50 of the British Nationality Act 1981 (c. 61) insert—

"50A Meaning of references to being in breach of immigration laws

(1) This section applies for the construction of a reference to being in the United Kingdom "in breach of the immigration laws" in—

(a) section 4(2) or (4);

(b) section 50(5); or

(c) Schedule 1.

(2) It applies only for the purpose of determining on or after the relevant day—

(a) whether a person born on or after the relevant day is a British citizen under section 1(1),

(b) whether, on an application under section 1(3) or 4(2) made on or after the relevant day, a person is entitled to be registered as a British citizen, or

(c) whether, on an application under section 6(1) or (2) made on or after the relevant day, the applicant fulfils the requirements of Schedule 1 for naturalisation as a British citizen under section 6(1) or (2).

(3) But that is subject to section 48(3)(d) and (4) of the Borders, Citizenship and Immigration Act 2009 (saving in relation to section 11 of the Nationality, Immigration and Asylum Act 2002).

(4) A person is in the United Kingdom in breach of the immigration laws if (and only if) the person—

(a) is in the United Kingdom;

(b) does not have the right of abode in the United Kingdom within the meaning of section 2 of the Immigration Act 1971;

(c) does not have leave to enter or remain in the United Kingdom (whether or not the person previously had leave);

(d) does not have a qualifying CTA entitlement;

(e) is not entitled to reside in the United Kingdom by virtue of any provision made under section 2(2) of the European Communities Act 1972 (whether or not the person was previously entitled);

(f) is not entitled to enter and remain in the United Kingdom by virtue of section 8(1) of the Immigration Act 1971 (crew) (whether or not the person was previously entitled); and

(g) does not have the benefit of an exemption under section 8(2) to (4) of that Act (diplomats, soldiers and other special cases) (whether or not the person previously had the benefit of an exemption).

(5) For the purposes of subsection (4)(d), a person has a qualifying CTA entitlement if the person—

(a) is a citizen of the Republic of Ireland,

(b) last arrived in the United Kingdom on a local journey (within the meaning of the Immigration Act 1971) from the Republic of Ireland, and

(c) on that arrival, was a citizen of the Republic of Ireland and was entitled to enter without leave by virtue of section 1(3) of the Immigration Act 1971 (entry from the common travel area).

(6) Section 11(1) of the Immigration Act 1971 (person deemed not to be in the United Kingdom before disembarkation, while in controlled area or while under immigration control) applies for the purposes of this section as it applies for the purposes of that Act.

(7) This section is without prejudice to the generality of—

(a) a reference to being in a place outside the United Kingdom in breach of immigration laws, and

(b) a reference in a provision other than one specified in subsection (1) to being in the United Kingdom in breach of immigration laws.

(8) The relevant day for the purposes of subsection (2) is the day appointed for the commencement of section 48 of the Borders, Citizenship and Immigration Act 2009 (which inserted this section)."

(2) Section 11 of the Nationality, Immigration and Asylum Act 2002 (c. 41) ("the 2002 Act") (unlawful presence in the United Kingdom) ceases to have effect.

(3) Notwithstanding its repeal, section 11 of the 2002 Act is to continue to have effect for the purpose of determining on or after the relevant day—

(a) whether a person born before the relevant day is a British citizen under section 1(1) of the British Nationality Act 1981 (c. 61),

(b) whether, on an application under section 1(3) or 4(2) of that Act made but not determined before the relevant day, a person is entitled to be registered as a British citizen,

(c) whether, on an application under section 6(1) or (2) of that Act made but not determined before the relevant day, the applicant fulfils the requirements of Schedule 1 for naturalisation as a British citizen under section 6(1) or (2) of that Act, or

(d) whether, in relation to an application under section 1(3) or 6(1) or (2) of that Act made on or after the relevant day, a person was in the United Kingdom "in breach of the immigration laws" at a time before 7 November 2002 (the date of commencement of section 11 of the 2002 Act).

(4) Where section 11 of the 2002 Act continues to have effect by virtue of paragraph (d) of subsection (3) for the purpose of determining on or after the relevant day the matter mentioned in that paragraph, section 50A of the British Nationality Act 1981 is not to apply for the purpose of determining that matter.

(5) The relevant day for the purposes of subsection (3) is the day appointed for the commencement of this section.

(6) In paragraph 7(a) of Schedule 3 to the 2002 Act (definition of persons unlawfully in the UK who are ineligible for support), for "section 11" substitute "section 50A of the British Nationality Act 1981".

49 Other interpretation etc.

(1) In section 50 of the British Nationality Act 1981 (c. 61) (interpretation), after subsection (1), insert—

"(1A) Subject to subsection (1B), references in this Act to being a member of the armed forces are references to being—

(a) a member of the regular forces within the meaning of the Armed Forces Act 2006, or

(b) a member of the reserve forces within the meaning of that Act subject to service law by virtue of paragraph (a), (b) or (c) of section 367(2) of that Act.

(1B) A person is not to be regarded as a member of the armed forces by virtue of subsection (1A) if the person is treated as a member of a regular or reserve force by virtue of—

(a) section 369 of the Armed Forces Act 2006, or

(b) section 4(3) of the Visiting Forces (British Commonwealth) Act 1933."

(2) In Schedule 1 to that Act (requirements for naturalisation as a British citizen), in paragraph 9(1), for "paragraph 2(b)" substitute "paragraph 2(1)(b) or 4(b)".

(3) After paragraph 10 of that Schedule insert—

"11 (1) This paragraph applies for the purposes of this Schedule.

(2) A person has qualifying temporary residence leave if—

(a) the person has limited leave to enter or remain in the United Kingdom, and

(b) the leave is granted for a purpose by reference to which a grant of probationary citizenship leave may be made.

(3) A person has probationary citizenship leave if—

(a) the person has limited leave to enter or remain in the United Kingdom, and

(b) the leave is of a description identified in rules under section 3 of the Immigration Act 1971 as "probationary citizenship leave",

and the reference in sub-paragraph (2) to a grant of probationary citizenship leave is to be construed accordingly.

(4) A person has permanent residence leave if the person has indefinite leave to enter or remain in the United Kingdom.

(5) A person has a qualifying CTA entitlement if the person—

(a) is a citizen of the Republic of Ireland,

(b) last arrived in the United Kingdom on a local journey (within the meaning of the Immigration Act 1971) from the Republic of Ireland, and

(c) on that arrival, was a citizen of the Republic of Ireland and was entitled to enter without leave by virtue of section 1(3) of the Immigration Act 1971 (entry from the common travel area).

(6) A person has a Commonwealth right of abode if the person has the right of abode in the United Kingdom by virtue of section 2(1)(b) of the Immigration Act 1971.

(7) A person has a permanent EEA entitlement if the person is entitled to reside in the United Kingdom permanently by virtue of any provision made under section 2(2) of the European Communities Act 1972.

(8) A person has a temporary EEA entitlement if the person does not have a permanent EEA entitlement but is entitled to reside in the United Kingdom by virtue of any provision made under section 2(2) of the European Communities Act 1972.

(9) A reference in this paragraph to having leave to enter or remain in the United Kingdom is to be construed in accordance with the Immigration Act 1971."

PART 3

IMMIGRATION

Studies

50 Restriction on studies

(1) In section 3(1)(c) of the Immigration Act 1971 (c. 77) (conditions that may be imposed on limited leave to enter or remain in the United Kingdom), after sub-paragraph (i) insert—

"(ia) a condition restricting his studies in the United Kingdom;".

(2) A condition under section 3(1)(c)(ia) of that Act may be added as a condition to leave given before the passing of this Act (as well as to leave given on or after its passing).

Fingerprinting

51 Fingerprinting of foreign criminals liable to automatic deportation

(1) Section 141 of the Immigration and Asylum Act 1999 (c. 33) (persons from whom fingerprints may be taken) is amended as follows.

(2) In subsection (7)(f), after "persons" insert ", other than a dependant of a person who falls within paragraph (c) by reason of a relevant immigration decision within subsection (16)(b) having been made in respect of that person".

(3) In subsection (16)—

(a) after "means" insert "—",

(b) the words from "a decision" to the end become paragraph (a), and

(c) after that paragraph insert ", or

(b) a decision that section 32(5) of the UK Borders Act 2007 applies (whether made before, or on or after, the day appointed for the commencement of section 51 of the Borders, Citizenship and Immigration Act 2009 which inserted this paragraph)".

Detention at ports in Scotland

52 Extension of sections 1 to 4 of the UK Borders Act 2007 to Scotland

(1) In section 2 of the UK Borders Act 2007 (c. 30) (detention at ports), after subsection (1), insert—

"(1A) A designated immigration officer at a port in Scotland may detain an individual if the immigration officer thinks that the individual is subject to a warrant for arrest."

(2) In section 3 of that Act (enforcement of detention at ports), after subsection (4), insert—

"(4A) In the application of this section to Scotland, the references in subsections (2)(a) and (3)(a) to 51 weeks shall be treated as references to 12 months."

(3) In section 60(1) of that Act (provisions which do not extend to Scotland), omit "1 to 4,".

PART 4

MISCELLANEOUS AND GENERAL

Judicial review

53 Transfer of certain immigration judicial review applications

(1) In section 31A of the Supreme Court Act 1981 (c. 54) (England and Wales: transfer from the High Court to the Upper Tribunal)—

(a) after subsection (2) insert—

"(2A) If Conditions 1, 2, 3 and 5 are met, but Condition 4 is not, the High Court must by order transfer the application to the Upper Tribunal.", and

(b) after subsection (7) insert—

"(8) Condition 5 is that the application calls into question a decision of the Secretary of State not to treat submissions as an asylum claim or a human rights claim within the meaning of Part 5 of the Nationality, Immigration and Asylum Act 2002 wholly or partly on the basis that they are not significantly different from material that has previously been considered (whether or not it calls into question any other decision)."

(2) In section 25A of the Judicature (Northern Ireland) Act 1978 (c. 23) (Northern Ireland: transfer from the High Court to the Upper Tribunal)—

(a) after subsection (2) insert—

"(2A) If Conditions 1, 2, 3 and 5 are met, but Condition 4 is not, the High Court must by order transfer the application to the Upper Tribunal.", and

(b) after subsection (7) insert—

"(8) Condition 5 is that the application calls into question a decision of the Secretary of State not to treat submissions as an asylum claim or a human rights claim within the meaning of Part 5 of the Nationality, Immigration and Asylum Act 2002 wholly or partly on the basis that they are not significantly different from material that has previously been considered (whether or not it calls into question any other decision)."

(3) In section 20 of the Tribunals, Courts and Enforcement Act 2007 (c. 15) (Scotland: transfer from the Court of Session to the Upper Tribunal)—

(a) in subsection (1), for the "and" at the end of paragraph (a) substitute—

"(aa) must, if Conditions 1, 2 and 5 are met, but Condition 4 is not, and", and

(b) after subsection (5) insert—

"(5A) Condition 5 is that the application calls into question a decision of the Secretary of State not to treat submissions as an asylum claim or a human rights claim within the meaning of Part 5 of the Nationality, Immigration and Asylum Act 2002 wholly or partly on the basis that they are not significantly different from material that has previously been considered (whether or not it calls into question any other decision)."

Trafficking people for exploitation

54 Trafficking people for exploitation

In section 4(4) of the Asylum and Immigration (Treatment of Claimants, etc.) Act 2004 (c. 19) (trafficking people for exploitation: meaning of exploitation), for paragraph (d) substitute—

"(d) a person uses or attempts to use him for any purpose within sub-paragraph (i), (ii) or (iii) of paragraph (c), having chosen him for that purpose on the grounds that—

(i) he is mentally or physically ill or disabled, he is young or he has a family relationship with a person, and

(ii) a person without the illness, disability, youth or family relationship would be likely to refuse to be used for that purpose."

Children

55 Duty regarding the welfare of children

(1) The Secretary of State must make arrangements for ensuring that—

(a) the functions mentioned in subsection (2) are discharged having regard to the need to safeguard and promote the welfare of children who are in the United Kingdom, and

(b) any services provided by another person pursuant to arrangements which are made by the Secretary of State and relate to the discharge of a function mentioned in subsection (2) are provided having regard to that need.

(2) The functions referred to in subsection (1) are—

(a) any function of the Secretary of State in relation to immigration, asylum or nationality;

(b) any function conferred by or by virtue of the Immigration Acts on an immigration officer;

(c) any general customs function of the Secretary of State;

(d) any customs function conferred on a designated customs official.

(3) A person exercising any of those functions must, in exercising the function, have regard to any guidance given to the person by the Secretary of State for the purpose of subsection (1).

(4) The Director of Border Revenue must make arrangements for ensuring that—

(a) the Director's functions are discharged having regard to the need to safeguard and promote the welfare of children who are in the United Kingdom, and

(b) any services provided by another person pursuant to arrangements made by the Director in the discharge of such a function are provided having regard to that need.

(5) A person exercising a function of the Director of Border Revenue must, in exercising the function, have regard to any guidance given to the person by the Secretary of State for the purpose of subsection (4).

(6) In this section—

"children" means persons who are under the age of 18;

"customs function", "designated customs official" and "general customs function" have the meanings given by Part 1.

(7) A reference in an enactment (other than this Act) to the Immigration Acts includes a reference to this section.

(8) Section 21 of the UK Borders Act 2007 (c. 30) (children) ceases to have effect.

General

56 Repeals

The Schedule contains repeals.

57 Extent

(1) Subject to the following provisions of this section, this Act extends to—

(a) England and Wales,

(b) Scotland, and

(c) Northern Ireland.

(2) Sections 22 (application of the PACE orders) and 23 (investigations and detention: England and Wales and Northern Ireland) extend to England and Wales and Northern Ireland only.

(3) An amendment, modification or repeal by this Act has the same extent as the enactment or relevant part of the enactment to which it relates (ignoring extent by virtue of an Order in Council under any of the Immigration Acts).

(4) Subsection (3) does not apply to—

(a) the amendments made by section 52 (detention at ports in Scotland);

(b) the amendment made by section 54 (trafficking people for exploitation), which extends to England and Wales and Northern Ireland only.

(5) Her Majesty may by Order in Council provide for any of the provisions of this Act, other than any provision of Part 1 (border functions) or section 53 (transfer of certain immigration judicial review applications), to extend, with or without modifications, to any of the Channel Islands or the Isle of Man.

(6) Subsection (5) does not apply in relation to the extension to a place of a provision which extends there by virtue of subsection (3).

58 Commencement

(1) Part 1 (border functions) comes into force on the day this Act is passed.

(2) The provisions of Part 2 (citizenship) come into force on such day as the Secretary of State may by order appoint.

(3) In Part 3 (immigration)—

(a) section 50 (restriction on studies) comes into force on the day this Act is passed;

(b) sections 51 (fingerprinting of foreign criminals) and 52 (detention at ports in Scotland) come into force on such day as the Secretary of State may by order appoint.

(4) In this Part—

(a) section 53 (transfer of certain immigration judicial review applications) comes into force on such day as the Lord Chancellor may by order appoint;

(b) sections 54 (trafficking people for exploitation) and 55 (duty regarding the welfare of children) come into force on such day as the Secretary of State may by order appoint.

(5) Any repeal in the Schedule (and section 56 so far as relating to the repeal) comes into force in the same way as the provisions of this Act to which the repeal relates.

(6) The other provisions of this Part come into force on the day this Act is passed.

(7) An order under this section must be made by statutory instrument.

(8) An order under this section—

(a) may appoint different days for different purposes;

(b) may include transitional or incidental provision or savings.

(9) An order commencing sections 39 to 41 (acquisition of British citizenship by naturalisation) must include provision that the amendments made by those sections do not have effect in relation to an application for naturalisation as a British citizen if—

(a) the date of the application is before the date on which those sections come into force in accordance with the order ("the date of commencement"), or

(b) the date of the application is before the end of the period of 24 months beginning with the date of commencement and the application is made by a person who falls within subsection (10) or (11).

(10) A person falls within this subsection if on the date of commencement the person has indefinite leave to remain in the United Kingdom.

(11) A person falls within this subsection if the person is given indefinite leave to remain in the United Kingdom on an application—

(a) the date of which is before the date of commencement, and

(b) which is decided after the date of commencement.

(12) The reference in subsection (9) to an order commencing sections 39 to 41 does not include an order commencing those sections for the purpose only of enabling regulations to be made under the British Nationality Act 1981 (c. 61).

(13) In the case of an order commencing sections 39 to 41, transitional provision may, in particular—

(a) provide that the qualifying period for the purposes of paragraph 1 or 3 of Schedule 1 to the British Nationality Act 1981 includes time before that commencement;

(b) provide for leave to enter or remain in the United Kingdom granted before that commencement to be treated as qualifying temporary residence leave or probationary citizenship leave for the purposes of that Schedule.

(14) In the case of an order commencing section 45 (acquisition of British citizenship through the female line), transitional provision may, in particular, provide that section 45 is to apply to an application made, but not determined, under section 4C of the British Nationality Act 1981 before that commencement.

(15) No order may be made commencing section 52 (detention at ports in Scotland) unless the Secretary of State has consulted the Scottish Ministers.

(16) No order may be made commencing section 53 (transfer of certain immigration judicial review applications) unless the functions of the Asylum and Immigration Tribunal in relation to appeals under Part 5 of the Nationality, Immigration and Asylum Act 2002 (c. 41) have been transferred under section 30(1) of the Tribunals, Courts and Enforcement Act 2007 (c. 15).

59 Short title

This Act may be cited as the Borders, Citizenship and Immigration Act 2009.

SCHEDULE

Section 56

REPEALS

PART 1

BORDER FUNCTIONS

Reference	*Extent of repeal*
UK Borders Act 2007 (c. 30)	Section 21(5)(a).
	In section 48— (a) in subsection (2), the words from the beginning to "Agency;", and (b) subsection (3).

PART 2

CITIZENSHIP

Reference	*Extent of repeal*
British Nationality Act 1981 (c. 61)	Section 3(4).
	In section 4B(1), the word "or" immediately before paragraph (c).
	In section 4C(2), the words "after 7th February 1961 and".
	In Schedule 1— (a) in paragraph 1(1)(a), the words from ", or the" to "this paragraph", (b) paragraph 1(3), and (c) paragraph 2(1)(c).
Hong Kong (War Wives and Widows) Act 1996 (c. 41)	In section 1(1), the word "and" immediately before paragraph (b).
Nationality, Immigration and Asylum Act 2002 (c. 41)	Section 11.
Immigration, Asylum and Nationality Act 2006 (c. 13)	Section 58.

PART 3

IMMIGRATION

Reference	*Extent of repeal*
UK Borders Act 2007 (c. 30)	In section 60(1), the words "1 to 4,".

PART 4

MISCELLANEOUS

Reference	*Extent of repeal*
UK Borders Act 2007 (c. 30)	Section 21.

GRANGIS - UK PUBLISHING 2022.

www.ingramcontent.com/pod-product-compliance
Lightning Source LLC
LaVergne TN
LVHW060214210926
848481LV00008B/2737